Cambridge English Readers

····································

Level 2

Series edit

The Dark Side of the City

Alan Battersby

CAMBRIDGE
UNIVERSITY PRESS

CAMBRIDGE
UNIVERSITY PRESS

University Printing House, Cambridge CB2 8BS, United Kingdom

Cambridge University Press is part of the University of Cambridge.

It furthers the University's mission by disseminating knowledge in the pursuit of education, learning and research at the highest international levels of excellence.

www.cambridge.org
Information on this title: www.cambridge.org/9781107635616

First published 2012
Reprinted 2015

Alan Battersby has asserted his right to be identified as the Author of the Work in accordance with the Copyright, Designs and Patents Act 1988.

Printed in the United Kingdom by Hobbs the Printers Ltd

Typeset by Aptara Inc.
Map artwork by Malcolm Barnes

A catalogue record for this publication is available from the British Library

ISBN 978-1-107-635616 Paperback

Contents

People in the story

Nat Marley: a New York private investigator

Curtis Wilson: a New York businessman

Stella Delgado: Nat Marley's personal assistant

Ellis Freeman: the owner of the pet store Animals International

Dionne Freeman: Ellis Freeman's wife and Curtis Wilson's sister

Joe Blaney: a colleague of Nat Marley, ex-NYPD (New York Police Department)

Mario Rossi: a friend of Nat Marley

Ed Winchester: a reporter on the *Daily News*

Grant and Tyler Gray: the owners of the software business Computer Kitchen

Captain Oldenberg: a detective with the NYPD

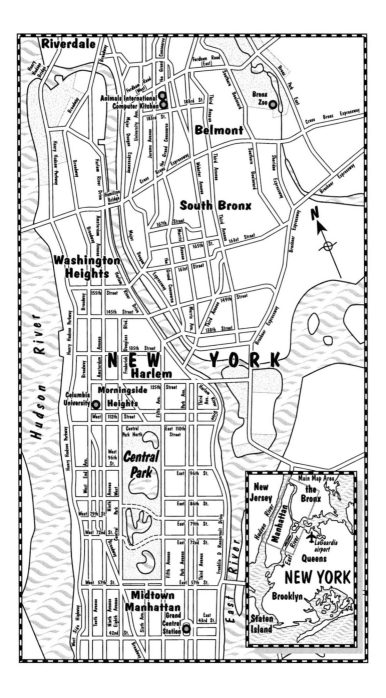

Chapter 1   *East 43rd Street, Manhattan*

Monday, January 17th. It was Martin Luther King Day, a holiday in the U.S.A. The streets of Manhattan were white with snow and unusually quiet. Many New Yorkers were enjoying a lazy long weekend with their families. But I don't have a family to spend time with, so I was working by myself at my office on East 43rd Street.

The name's Nat Marley. I've been a private investigator in this city for over ten years. Before that, I was a police officer with the New York Police Department, "an NYPD cop." The working life of an investigator is rather different from what you see in the movies – I'm not often in danger. Maybe a wife wants to know if her husband's seeing another woman. Or sometimes I'm looking for a teenager who's run away from home.

While I was working, I got a phone call.

"Nat Marley speaking," I said.

"I'm pleased I caught you on a holiday. My name's Curtis Wilson," the caller began. "I want to talk with you about a family problem, but not over the phone. Could I see you this afternoon?"

"Sure. I could meet with you at two o'clock," I replied.

January can be a quiet month for business, so I hoped this man was going to be a rich new client.

Wilson arrived just after two o'clock, his smart coat white with snow. He was tall and good-looking – unlike me –

and his clothes were expensive. He looked like the sort of man who knows what he wants in life and how to get it. I also thought I knew his face from somewhere. Then I remembered a name from the past – Bad Boy Bronx. That was his name when he was a famous hip-hop musician.

"I know your face, Mr. Wilson," I said. "I guess you don't do much rapping now."

"You're right," he laughed. "I've come a long way in life since I was a kid in South Bronx. Things are different now. I make more money from my businesses than I ever did from music. The banks open their doors when they see Curtis Wilson coming."

"So you have a family problem?" I asked.

"Yeah, my sister Dionne is worried about her husband, Ellis Freeman," he replied. "In the last few months, she's seen a real change in him. He's just not the same man. Something's happened, but he won't talk about it."

"Tell me more," I said. "How has he changed?"

"He was always full of fun and loved to laugh and joke," said Wilson. "But Dionne doesn't see that side of him now. She says he seems worried all the time. But he does his work as usual."

"What does your brother-in-law do?" I asked.

"Ellis and Dionne have a pet store called Animals International on the Grand Concourse in the Bronx. You can find everything there from birds to snakes," said Wilson.

"An interesting kind of business. But could they have money problems?" I asked.

"I asked Dionne the same question," Wilson answered. "She told me that doing business has gotten more difficult, but they make enough money."

"Are there any other problems between them?" I asked. "Do they get along well?"

"Dionne couldn't be married to a better guy," said Wilson.

"What happens when Dionne asks him why he's worried?" I asked.

"He just won't say anything. She thinks he could be afraid of something – or someone," Wilson replied.

"I'll tell you what I could do. I'll visit their store tomorrow morning and see what I can find out."

"OK, but do it carefully," said Wilson. "I don't want Ellis to know that his brother-in-law is paying an investigator. He likes to do things his way."

"Sure, I understand," I said. "Do you have a photo of them I could have?"

Wilson passed me a picture of the Freemans. They looked like any other happy husband and wife. I thought for a moment and decided what to do.

"I have an idea," I said. "When I visit the store I'll let them think I'm interested in buying a snake. I'll get them talking and see what happens."

Chapter 2 *The Grand Concourse, the Bronx*

Tuesday, January 18th. I left my apartment on Main Street, Queens. The soft snow on the sidewalks was changing to hard ice and the wind cut like a knife against my face. I walked carefully to the subway station, where I took a number seven train to Grand Central Station. In New York I prefer taking public transportation to cabs – it's both quicker and cheaper.

As I left Grand Central I looked up, but couldn't see the top of the Chrysler Building. It was somewhere above the heavy snow clouds. Five minutes later I was at my office. My personal assistant, Stella Delgado, was already at her desk. She looked up from her computer.

"Morning, Nat. Is it cold enough for you?" she asked.

"I've known worse winters than this," I laughed.

"You know, Nat, my computer's getting so slow! When are you going to buy me a new one?" she asked.

"When our new client pays me lots of money. Not before," I replied.

Stella has worked for me since I started as an investigator. She's a smart, good-looking Puerto Rican who knows a lot more than me about computers. With her help, I can always do my job better. She gave me a strange look when I said, "I got to see a man about a snake." Then I told her all about our new client and his family problem.

Later that morning I traveled uptown on a number four train from Grand Central to 183rd Street in the Bronx. From there it was a short walk to the Grand Concourse, a main street that runs north to south across the Bronx. You can find everything in the Bronx. In the south there are poorer areas with real problems. In the center and the north you can find more parks and gardens than in all of Manhattan.

The Freemans' pet store was one in a line of stores and businesses along the Grand Concourse. Inside there was the warm smell of animals and the sound of birds singing. A woman in a store coat came and asked if I needed any help. She had a soft voice and a kind smile. I remembered her from the photo – Dionne Freeman.

I had my story ready. "Sure," I replied. "It's my son's ninth birthday soon. He's asked for a new pet, but nothing like a dog or a cat. He wants something interesting and different, like a snake. Nothing dangerous, of course – one that's safe with children. Do you have any ideas?"

"Why don't you talk with my husband?" she asked. "He knows much more than me about snakes. I'll take you through to the back room."

Inside the room, the first thing I saw were tanks with glass fronts and sides. I knew almost nothing about the different snakes inside them. A guy with glasses and short dark hair was giving the snakes their food.

"Ellis!" Dionne called. "Could you help choose a snake for this man's young son?"

"Pleased to meet you," he said to me. "Meet my snakes. Aren't they beautiful?"

Beautiful wasn't what I was thinking, but I wanted to be friendly. "Yeah, they sure are lovely," I replied.

"So it'll be your son's first snake, huh?" asked Freeman. "Take a look at this one. It's a Kenyan sand boa. It's not dangerous and it's really good with children. It's what we call a beginner's snake."

"So it's come here all the way from Africa?" I asked.

"No!" laughed Freeman. "This baby was born right here in this store."

Inside the tank there was a small yellow and brown snake which wasn't moving. It had to be asleep or dead. Or was it just bored with life?

"Watch this," said Freeman. "Dinner time! Come and get it!"

He put a dead mouse in the tank. The snake moved quickly and took the animal in its mouth. Then in just a few seconds it was "goodbye mouse."

"Now it won't want anything for another two weeks," said Freeman, smiling at the snake.

"I'm sure my kid will love it," I said. "So how much does a snake like this cost?"

"This one's a hundred dollars, and then you'll need the tank and other things. That will come to about three hundred dollars," Freeman told me.

"I'll have to think about that," I replied. "And I don't have a car – how could I get it home to Queens?"

"No problem," said Freeman. "I can bring it over in the van. I go out two or three times a week – I take people their new pets, and bring pet food to old clients. Some rich New Yorkers never have time to shop for pet food. And all pets need to have just the right sort of food, like mice for the snakes. Tomorrow's going to be a busy day. I'll be on the road early, taking food to clients around the Bronx and Manhattan."

"So business is good then?" I asked.

"Well, it's not easy with all the other pet stores in the Bronx, but we're doing OK."

"Well, thanks for your time and help," I said. "I'll talk to my wife about it and let you know."

The store was warm and comfortable. But outside it was below zero and snow was falling again. I called Wilson on my cellphone and told him about my visit to the store. "I didn't see anything strange," I said. "It looked like business as usual."

"So what next?" asked Wilson.

"Tomorrow Freeman is driving around the Bronx and Manhattan, taking pet food to his clients," I began. "I'm going to follow him and watch what he does and where he goes. Maybe I'll find out something more interesting."

As I walked back to the subway station, it felt colder than ever. And it wasn't just the snow – I wasn't feeling too good at all. January – what a great time to catch a cold!

Chapter 3   *On the road*

Wednesday, January 19th. When I woke up at five thirty I felt terrible, but I couldn't stay in bed. I had a client to keep happy. Before going out into the cold dark morning, there was just time for a quick coffee. An old NYPD friend, Joe Blaney, was waiting outside for me in his car. Years ago, Joe taught me more about police work than any teacher at the police academy. He's the sort of guy who helps you feel safe when you're in danger. He doesn't work for the NYPD any more, but sometimes helps me with an investigation. I asked Joe to wait while I bought some things from the 24/7 store along the street. Then, with aspirins and a box of paper handkerchiefs, I was ready to start my day.

From Queens, Joe drove north across the East River to the Bronx. New snow on the road meant he had to go slowly. In the warm car I fell asleep for a time. Joe woke me as we arrived at the Grand Concourse. He passed the Freemans' store and stopped under some trees. I turned in my seat and watched the pet store. Nobody was around yet.

Around six forty-five, Ellis Freeman arrived in a white van. I saw him unlock the door of the pet store, then the lights went on inside. Soon he was busy carrying boxes and his green and yellow pet store bags to the van. I took pictures of him as he worked. When he finished he stood waiting next to the van.

"What's he doing?" asked Joe. "Did he forget something?"

"No idea," I replied. "Let's wait and see."

Soon we had our answer. After looking up and down the street, Freeman spoke into his cellphone. Two young guys came out of a door a short way down the street. Both guys were carrying bags in each hand. They went over to the back of the van and Freeman helped them put the bags inside.

"See those bags, Joe?" I asked. "They're like the green and yellow bags that Freeman uses in his store."

"Yeah," Joe replied. "But these bags have a red line around them."

The two guys were now talking with Freeman. I couldn't hear what they were saying, but Freeman looked angry and uncomfortable. This wasn't a conversation between friends.

"Take a good look at those two guys. Are they brothers?" asked Joe.

They both had the same blonde hair, the same eyes and thin mouths. When I looked from one to the other again, I understood. "Not just brothers, Joe," I said, "They have to be twins."

At last Freeman drove off. It was seven fifteen and it was beginning to get light. The van wasn't difficult to follow. We could see the words "Animals International" in large letters on the back doors. Freeman started by leaving bags and boxes at addresses in Belmont, a big Italian-American area of the Bronx. Then he drove north and did the same in richer, greener areas of the Bronx like Riverdale. Time passed slowly as we watched. Sometimes Freeman spent a long time in a building, maybe talking to his clients. So far I could see nothing unusual. But I wrote down all the addresses.

My box of paper handkerchiefs was now half-empty. Joe looked at me with a friendly smile. "That cold's getting worse," he said. "You need to be in bed."

From Riverdale, Freeman took the West Side Highway and drove south to Manhattan. It was snowing heavily again, so nobody was moving fast. As we went across the Henry Hudson Bridge, I couldn't see New Jersey over the gray waters of the Hudson River. Freeman went ahead with his work again, leaving bags at addresses in north Manhattan. We could see that there weren't many bags and boxes left in the van now.

Soon Freeman was driving through Morningside Heights. He stopped on West 112th Street and took the last bag, one with a red line around it, from the van. He walked across the street to number 52 and rang the bell to one of the apartments. There was a sign outside the building about an apartment for rent. Two minutes later Freeman was still standing outside the building. It looked like nobody was at home. Freeman waited another minute, then took the bag back to his van and drove away.

I felt sick and was tired, but we had a job to finish. "Joe, keep following Freeman," I said. "I have an idea." I took out my phone and made a call.

"Good morning, Westside Apartments," replied a woman. "How can I help you?"

"I see you have an apartment to rent at 52, West 112th Street," I began. "It looks just right, but I need to know if I could keep pets there."

"I'm very sorry, sir, but we don't allow pets in any apartment in that building," she said.

"Oh, come on! What about a little snake?" I asked, smiling.

"Certainly not!" she said, as she put the phone down.

"That's odd," I said to Joe. "Why did Freeman try to leave a bag at a place where you can't keep pets?"

As we followed Freeman back to the Bronx, Joe said, "Boss, you've had enough for one day. You look half-dead."

"You're right, Joe," I replied. "But we can't stop now. I have to see what happens when Freeman gets back to the store."

When Freeman stopped on the Grand Concourse, he took the last bag from his van and walked down to the door down the street. It was the same door that the twins came out of earlier. He went inside, but two minutes later he was standing back on the street. Then he tried to make a call on his cellphone. It looked like nobody was answering. Freeman looked tired and angry as he went back to his store with the bag.

"Joe, get yourself some lunch and meet me back here," I said. "I'm going to see where that door goes."

I found it between two stores – it was open and inside were stairs leading up to a second-floor office. There was a sign above the office door with the name of the business: "Computer Kitchen – Cooking New Ideas." I tried opening the door, but it was locked.

I went down to Joe's car and waited until he came back from lunch. Then I told him what I wanted him to do.

"I'm afraid it's going to be a long, boring afternoon. Could you watch Freeman's store? I have to know if Freeman sees those twins again, or takes that bag back to them. Call me the moment you see anything. I'm going to the office to get some rest."

Chapter 4   *Locks and keys*

It was early afternoon when I arrived back at the office in East 43rd Street. Stella wasn't at all pleased when she saw how sick I was.

"Nat! Why don't you stay home?" she asked. "You really don't look good."

"I know, Stella," I replied. "But it's one of those days when I can't stop. I got to make some calls and then I'll get some sleep. I'll feel better after that."

Stella gave me a look which meant: "I don't believe you."

First, I called Curtis Wilson. After telling him about my morning's work, I said, "I'm not sure what Freeman is doing, but I don't like what I saw. I'll see what I can find out about those guys who gave him the bags. And I got someone watching the store this afternoon. If Freeman doesn't come out with that last bag, I'll take a look around the store – after closing time."

"How will you do that?" asked Wilson.

"I know a guy whose business is opening locked doors," I said.

The guy I was thinking about was Mario Rossi. Years ago he was one of the city's bad guys. He didn't need a key to open a lock. He could get through any door or window, no problem. Now he has a store in the East Village where he sells locks and keys. From time to time I've helped him, but now I needed his help. A quick call was enough to get what I wanted.

"Hi, Mario? Nat Marley here," I began. "I need some help. I have to look around a store. After closing time, if you see what I mean."

Mario quickly understood what I meant. I told him what I wanted.

"OK, Nat. I'll wait for your call this evening," said Mario. "I could drive over to your office. Then I'll take you to the Bronx."

I told Stella to wake me at six. I drank a large Scotch from the office bottle and made myself comfortable on the sofa. In a few minutes I fell asleep.

I was having a wonderful dream when Stella woke me. I was dreaming that I had an office at the top of the Chrysler Building. The richest and most beautiful women in New York were my clients, and I had millions of dollars in the bank. Sometimes waking up can be too sad.

"How are you feeling, Nat?" Stella asked.

"I could be worse," I replied. "Earlier I felt half-dead, but now I'm only a quarter-dead."

"Well, if you can joke, you must be getting better," she laughed. "And I've heard nothing from Joe."

At seven o'clock, Joe gave me the news I needed. The pet store was now closed and Freeman went home without that important bag. So it must still be inside. Then I phoned Rossi. "OK, Mario, let's go ahead," I said.

Rossi arrived soon after seven thirty. He's a small Italian-American guy with almost no hair. Rossi drove me uptown to the Bronx along Third Avenue. It wasn't the best time to travel anywhere fast in this city. People were trying to hurry home and the roads were busy and slow. It was almost eight thirty by the time we got to the Freemans' pet store.

Rossi got out of the car and went over to take a quick look at the locks.

When he came back he was smiling. "They got locks that my twelve-year-old daughter could get through," he told me. "I'll get my things. Watch the street while I work on the door."

Rossi easily unlocked the door and we went inside. In the front of the store, there was enough light from the streetlights outside to see around. But we didn't find the bag or anything unusual there. Then we moved through to the back room, where Freeman kept his snakes. Here it was safe to use flashlights.

"We're looking for a yellow and green store bag with a red line around it," I told Rossi.

"OK, Nat," he replied. "What's behind these big boxes? Let's take a look."

The boxes were empty, so they were easy to move. Behind them was another door for Rossi to unlock. This time, he found the job was more difficult, but he did it after five minutes. The last room was smaller and inside there were more glass tanks. I couldn't see anything inside them. The room was quiet until I heard a loud noise from one of the tanks.

"What on earth was that?" I asked.

"It's a rattlesnake," said Rossi. "They make that noise when you get too near."

"That's strange," I thought. "A rattlesnake in New York? I thought you couldn't keep dangerous snakes like that here."

I got out my camera and took some pictures of the rattlesnake. The other tanks were empty.

In a corner under a tank was a cupboard. Mario got down on his knees and unlocked it. And there was a yellow and green bag with a red line around it. I opened this bag carefully with my pocket knife. Inside there were four small plastic bags with something white in them.

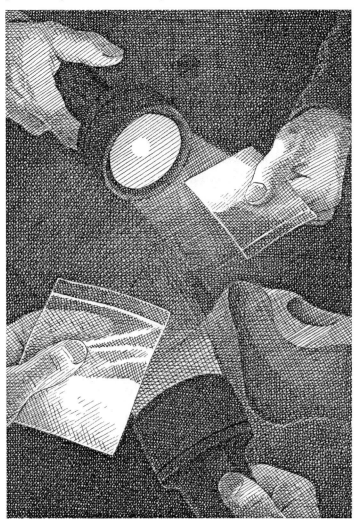

"Is this what I think it is, Nat?" asked Mario.

"Right first time. Drugs – probably cocaine," I replied. "I'll take some pictures, then we're out of here fast!"

I put everything carefully back into the bag. We were almost ready to leave when Mario said, "On the floor! Quick!"

"What's wrong?" I asked quietly.

"There's a police car coming very slowly along the street," he answered. "Don't move and keep quiet!"

We stayed on the floor for a minute. Then Mario looked outside carefully. The danger was over. "Come on, let's move," he said.

When we were back inside the car, Mario asked, "Nat, you want to eat? We're not far from Belmont and the finest Italian restaurants in this town."

I was more interested in hot coffee, a warm bed and a long sleep. "Sorry. I'll have to say thanks, but no thanks," I said. "I don't feel too good, so let's do dinner another day, huh? Could you take me back to Queens?"

Back at my apartment I made coffee and watched the news on TV. A reporter began: "This is Cindy Lu speaking to you from Morningside Heights on the Upper West Side. Early this morning, police found the body of a man in his twenties, in an apartment near Columbia University. So far, the police can't say how the man died. Other people in the building say there was a party in the apartment last night, but they didn't hear anything unusual."

I thought about the story. Morningside Heights is a safe area and home to many of the teachers at Columbia University. And people don't usually die at parties, not at the parties I go to anyway.

Chapter 5   *Snakes and drugs*

Thursday, January 20th. When I woke up I felt a little better. I looked out at the sky and for the first time in a week saw small windows of blue between the heavy gray clouds. At last a change in the weather.

Stella phoned and wanted to know how I was feeling. "Not so bad – well, better than yesterday," I said. "Look, I'm going to be late. Were there any calls for me?"

"Yes. Curtis Wilson wants to meet with you here. Can you make it for eleven?" she asked.

"No problem," I replied. "See you later."

I had almost nothing to eat the day before, so I needed a real breakfast. I washed and dressed and walked along Main Street to Slim Pete's Diner.

"Hi there, Mr. Marley. What can I do for New York's most famous investigator?" asked Pete. There's nothing slim about Pete – he's a big man who clearly enjoys his own cooking.

"First, not too many jokes, if you don't mind," I said. "And second, coffee, toast, bacon and eggs. Keep the coffee coming, will you?"

As I ate, I looked through the *Daily News*. I found something new on the Morningside Heights story. The dead man was called Ross Gallagher and he was taking cocaine at the party. But the drug was much stronger than the usual cocaine people buy on the street. And he drank a lot of alcohol at the party – the cocaine and alcohol together became a killer.

I thought about the drug problem in the city. When people buy cocaine, they have little idea what they're really buying. They don't know how weak or how strong the drug is or what else is in it. When people start taking cocaine, they think it's just fun. But then they can't stop themselves – it's like living in a locked room which you can't escape from.

Then I thought about the bag Mario and I found last night in the pet store – the bag Freeman tried to leave in West 112th Street yesterday morning. Morningside Heights. I hoped it wasn't the same address.

When I arrived at my office, I gave Stella my camera. "Will you put these photos on the computer?" I asked. "And could you print them out for myself and for Mr. Wilson?"

While Stella was working on the photos, I called an old friend, Ed Winchester, at the *Daily News*. He's been a reporter on the paper for years.

"How are you doing, Nat?" he asked. "Will I see you in McFadden's Bar around lunchtime?"

"Sorry, Ed. I'm too busy today," I said. "But I need your help. Could you find me the address in Morningside Heights where Ross Gallagher died at that party?"

"Sure. I'll call you back soon," said Ed.

Later, when Stella had the photos ready, I looked through them. "You see these pictures of a snake," I said. "I know it's some kind of rattlesnake, but since I know almost zero about snakes …"

"OK, I'll find out what it is," said Stella.

When Wilson arrived, I took him through to my office. "I'm afraid it's not good news," I began.

"OK. Let's hear it," he said.

As I told Wilson the story, I showed him the pictures: "Here you can see the two guys giving bags to Freeman."

"I've never seen these men before. And Ellis sure doesn't look happy," said Wilson.

"Then we followed Freeman as he took pet food to his clients," I said. "We know he tried to leave a bag at a building where they don't allow pets. But no one was in, so he took it back to the store. Now things get worse. These photos show what I found inside that bag in Freeman's store last night. I'm sure there were drugs inside the other bags that the two guys gave Freeman."

As Wilson looked at the pictures his mouth fell open, but he didn't speak. Then he put his head in his hands and said, "I can't believe it. What has Ellis gotten himself into?"

Before I could reply, Ed Winchester called back: "I have what you want, Nat," he said. "The address is 52, West 112th. But I couldn't get the apartment number – the police won't say."

"Thanks, Ed," I said. "Next time I see you, I'll buy you a beer."

"More bad news," I said to Wilson. "You know the Morningside Heights story – where a man died after taking drugs at a party? Yesterday Freeman tried to leave a bag in the same building on West 112th Street."

"So maybe it was the same apartment …" Wilson began.

I stopped him: "We just don't know, but I really hope not."

"What happens now?" asked Wilson.

"We need to know more about the guys who gave Ellis the bags," I replied. "I'll visit their office this afternoon. I'll call you when I have something more to tell you."

After Wilson left, I looked on the internet to find out more about Computer Kitchen, the business near Freeman's store. On their website I found pictures of the guys who gave the bags to Freeman – Grant and Tyler Gray. I read that they were busy thinking up the next big ideas in computers.

Stella came into my office. She looked really worried and I could see that she had a problem.

"Nat, I'm not sure if I did the right thing," she began. "It was difficult looking at pictures of snakes on the internet. I couldn't find one that looked like the snake in your photos. So I emailed your pictures to the Bronx Zoo. They just emailed back. It's an Aruba Island rattlesnake, from the Caribbean. They're very interested to know where you got the pictures because this snake is in danger. You can't bring them into this country."

28

Chapter 6 *Snakes and computers*

Freeman was in big trouble. First, we found drugs in his store, and now we knew he also had a dangerous snake there. He didn't want the cops to know about the rattlesnake, that was for sure.

"Don't worry, Stella," I said. "You've done a great job. I'll make sure the Bronx Zoo doesn't start asking questions. But right now I need your help again."

When I told Wilson, "I'll visit their office" that wasn't quite true. Actually, I wanted Stella to visit them. Stella can do some jobs much better than me. Talking intelligently about computers is one of them.

I told Stella what I wanted. "Talk to the guys. Let them think you're an important businesswoman who's looking for smart guys with new ideas. See how much they really know. I want to find out if this is a real business or something different. Also, I need to know what sort of people they are."

"OK, Nat," she replied, giving me a half-smile. "But you know I don't feel good about doing this sort of work. What if something goes wrong?"

"I'll only be a few doors away," I said. "I'll wait down the street and if there's a problem, call me."

We walked out into the cold air. There was more blue in the sky over Manhattan and almost no wind. From Grand Central we took a number four train to the Bronx. Later, as we walked along the Grand Concourse, I told Stella, "I know you can do it. You'll be better at this job than a car full of cops. When you finish, find me in the 99-cent store along the street. It's warmer in there than on the street."

I knew things were OK when she found me forty-five minutes later. There was a big smile on her face.

"That was so strange, Nat," she began. "I don't think those guys are living in the real world. All their ideas are things other people have already done. They showed me a program called Song Bird – they said it was a new idea for texting friends on cellphones. It's nothing new. It's like they're a year behind everyone else in the business."

"What did you think of them as people?" I asked.

"I can't say I liked them," she said. "They look like students from an expensive New England college. And another thing – I think they found it difficult to talk to a woman. I didn't like the way they looked at me. There was something cold in their eyes."

"So if they're not making any money …" I began.

"Well, that's where you're wrong, Nat," she said. "I was looking around their office – beautiful furniture and expensive computers. Maybe you could buy me one like that. It's a …"

"Stop right there, Stella!" I said. "I'm not spending anything on computers until Wilson pays me."

On the opposite side of the Grand Concourse there was a large store called World of Computers. Maybe the people working there could tell us a little more about the Gray twins.

"You've given me an idea," I said. "Come on, let's do some shopping over there. There must be some things you need for the office – except for a new computer."

By spending a few dollars I hoped I could also ask some questions. When I was ready to pay the saleswoman, I started a conversation. "Say, do you know those two guys named Gray from Computer Kitchen across the street?" I asked.

"Oh, they come in from time to time," she said. "The boss told me about them. They both studied at Columbia University and now they're hoping to become the next Microsoft Corporation. They'll be lucky!"

It was time to call Wilson and tell him what I knew about the rattlesnake and the Grays. Before I could speak, Wilson had some bad news for me.

"Thanks for calling, Mr. Marley," he began. "Look, I just heard from Dionne Freeman. Things have gone from bad to worse. Ellis went out at lunchtime today, and when he came back to the store there was blood on his face. He was hurt quite badly. Ellis told her it was a street robbery. Of course Dionne wanted to call 911, but Ellis didn't let her."

"I'm very sorry to hear that," I said. "Look, I have something more on those guys with the computer business along the street. I could be wrong, but I don't think they're very interested in the computer business. They're smart – they were Columbia University students – but their ideas aren't new. My guess is that the computer business is just a front. I think they're making their real money from selling drugs."

"Snakes and drugs don't go together. What is Ellis doing in this dirty business?" asked Wilson. "Does he have money problems or is it something else?"

"There's one way to find out," I said. "I have to talk with Freeman … I need to get him away from his wife. If I could get him someplace by himself, someplace where he'll agree to come … When I was in his store on Tuesday, I asked him about a snake for my son. I'll ask him to bring it over to my apartment on Main Street, Queens. I'll see if he can do it tomorrow."

"You want me to be there too?" asked Wilson. "It's time for Ellis to know how his family feels. I guess he won't like it, but he needs to know what we're doing for him."

"Thanks. I'm sure I'll need help," I said. "Freeman doesn't

know me well, so probably won't tell me everything. I think he'll talk to you. I'll call you when I know the time."

I told Stella she could go back to the office. I had more shopping to do. This time it was for a snake. I went into Animals International, where the Freemans remembered me.

"I hope you're going to make that son of yours a happy boy," said Dionne Freeman with a big smile.

"I sure am," I replied. "I want the snake and everything else. Now it's his birthday on Saturday, so could you bring it all over tomorrow while he's in school? But are you going to be OK to drive?" I asked, looking at Freeman's face.

"No problem. I'll be fine. Queens, wasn't it?" asked Ellis Freeman. "I can do it early afternoon around two o'clock. And since it's his birthday, I'll give him something too." He went over to a cupboard and took out a thin book. "Here you are. It's all about snakes, written for kids."

I felt really bad. The story about a son and his birthday was all untrue and these people were being kind to me. But I had to do it. I gave Freeman my name and full address. Tomorrow I could question him.

Chapter 7   *Real answers*

Friday, January 21st. The weather was still getting better and so was I. Now I didn't feel like a wet towel that someone left on the bathroom floor. It was above zero and there were blue skies over Queens. Maybe spring was coming early. It can be like that in New York sometimes. Winter one day, spring the next.

I had a few things to do at my office before meeting with Freeman at my apartment. I needed the photos of Freeman at work, the Aruba Island rattlesnake and the drugs. But first I had to call the Bronx Zoo.

"This is Nat Marley. My personal assistant emailed some pictures of an Aruba Island rattlesnake to you yesterday … No, there's nothing wrong here, no problem … It's just that my son's studying snakes at school, and he found the photos on some website about animals in danger. He wanted to know what sort of snake it was, so I asked my assistant to email the pictures to you. That's all, nothing more."

I hoped they believed my story and didn't tell the cops. I really didn't want a visit from the NYPD.

I went back to my apartment in Queens, and met with Curtis Wilson at one thirty. I showed him into the kitchen, where he could wait until I called him. Then I made coffee and took it into the lounge. Soon after two o'clock, Freeman's van stopped outside the building. I ran downstairs to talk with him before he could open the back doors of the van.

"Good to see you again, Mr. Freeman," I said. "Now, before we take anything up to the apartment, why don't we agree on the best place to put the tank?"

"Why not?" replied Freeman. "Remember, snakes like to be away from the sun."

When Freeman was inside the apartment, I invited him into the living room to sit down. "I just made coffee. Like a cup?" I asked.

While we drank the coffee, Freeman talked to me about snakes. "If you take the snake out of the tank, always watch where it goes," he said. "I once had a client who lost her snake in her apartment. She didn't find it until a week later, under some clothes in her bedroom closet."

He got up. "So, let's find the best place for the tank. Can you show me your son's room?"

"Stay there a minute," I told him. "I got something to show you."

I took the photos of the Grays and the drugs out of my bag and gave them to Freeman. He sat down again and looked at each picture. Then he looked up at me with large sad eyes.

"Who are you and what do you want from me?" he asked in a quiet voice.

"I am Nat Marley. That's true. But I'm afraid there's no son or birthday," I replied, showing him my investigator's I.D. "I'm working for someone in your family. He's been worried about you. He wants answers. He wants to know what's happening."

Freeman looked down at the floor and asked, "You going to tell the police?"

"I know enough to call the police right now. But I'm not going to do that. With your family's help, we're going to find answers to your problems. Your brother-in-law wants to talk with you. Come on in, Mr. Wilson," I called.

"Curtis!" said Freeman, looking up as Wilson came in. "I'm sorry. I really didn't want the family to know about this. I tried to do everything my way, but it didn't work. Now I hate myself."

Wilson put his hands on Freeman's shoulders and said, "Ellis, it looks like you made some big mistakes. Dionne tried to talk to you. She called me because she didn't know what to do. That's when I asked Mr. Marley to help."

"You must tell us everything, Mr. Freeman," I said. "The full story."

"OK. This is going to hurt Dionne, but I'll do it," said Freeman. "Curtis, you remember that Dionne had to go into the hospital about two years ago?"

"That's right," replied Wilson. "She needed a big operation."

"Well, that was how all my problems began," said Freeman. "Like any good husband, I saved money every month for doctor's and hospital bills. But I didn't save enough to pay for the best hospital, and Dionne's life was in danger. So without telling her, I borrowed from the bank. What else could I do?"

"Why didn't you come to me for help?" asked Wilson.

"I believe a man has to find the answers to his own problems and look after his family," said Freeman.

"You're a good man," said Wilson, "but you made life difficult for yourself."

"The next problem was how to pay back $50,000 to the bank," said Freeman. "I started another business which Dionne knew nothing about – buying and selling snakes that the U.S.A. doesn't allow into the country. In the beginning, I just sold to old clients. If you know what you're doing, it's not too difficult to bring snakes into the country. As I got more business and new clients, I knew I could soon pay back the bank. But I had to keep everything from Dionne – how could I tell her what I was doing?"

"So how did things go wrong?" I asked.

"You know, some people who keep dangerous snakes are kind of dangerous themselves," said Freeman. "And two of those are the Gray twins."

"So they bought a snake from you?" I asked.

"Yeah. About a year ago," said Freeman. "They wanted a Burmese python and I got a good price for it. Then, three months later, the Grays invited me to their office. I thought they wanted to buy another snake, but I was wrong.

"They said, 'Let's watch a movie,' and laughed. The 'movie' was me selling them the Burmese python and taking the money. They had it all on camera. I had to agree to take their drugs on my van. I can remember what they said: 'Our new business is growing fast and we need help. Be a good boy and do what we say. Or we send our home movie to the NYPD.'"

"When did you learn what was in the bags?" I asked.

"Very soon," said Freeman, "and I felt terrible about what I was doing. I couldn't tell Dionne, but she knew something was wrong. I thought things couldn't get worse, but then I saw the news story about Ross Gallagher. The Grays gave me a bag for an apartment at 52 West 112th Street every week, and that's the building where Gallagher died. I don't know for sure if he died because of the Grays' drugs. But I knew I had to stop."

"There never was a street robbery yesterday, was there?" Wilson asked.

"No. I went round to see the Grays at lunchtime and said I couldn't take their bags any more. Their answer was to hit me hard in the face. They said, 'You want your pretty wife to get the same?'"

With the new information from Freeman I could now put together all the pieces of the story. The problem was how to help Freeman. Was there a way out?

"Mr. Freeman, I understand how difficult this must be. But thank you for telling us everything."

"You know, I feel a lot better just for talking," said Freeman. "It's the first time I've told anyone."

"When do the Grays want you to take their drugs out on your van again?" I asked.

"Tomorrow morning, same time as usual," Freeman replied.

"Right, I need to think of what to do. But now I want you to go back to your store. For the moment it's still business as usual with the Grays. And one more thing, Mr. Freeman. The buying and selling of dangerous snakes has to stop. We have to get that rattlesnake out of your store as soon as possible. I'll be round later to get it. Make sure it's ready."

As Freeman left, Wilson spoke to him. "Ellis, you have the most important job of your life to do. When you see Dionne, you have to tell her everything. Be a good husband. You need her and she needs you."

I showed Freeman to the door and turned to Wilson.

"I need a drink. How about you?" I said.

"Sure," he replied. "Scotch with soda, please."

I made the drinks, sat down with Wilson and told him what I thought.

"Freeman has made a terrible mistake. And so have the Grays. I don't believe they understand the real dangers of selling drugs. They say their business is growing fast. So they're taking lots of money away from other people selling drugs. Sooner or later they'll get a visit from the big boys in the drug business. And that won't be good news."

"And what about Ellis? Is he in danger too from the 'big boys,' as you call them?" said Wilson.

"Maybe," I answered. "So we need to do something quickly. In the end the police have to know," I said. "But for the moment I don't want to make things more difficult for Freeman. I need to stop the Grays from using Freeman. And I have to make sure there's nothing that could lead the police to him. The question is how. I need some time to think. I'll call you later."

When Wilson left I called Joe.

"Joe, I need your help. I got a snake who needs a ride to the Bronx Zoo," I said. "I'll tell you about it on the way."

I had to be sure that there were no more dangerous snakes at Freeman's pet store. And I had to think of a good story to tell them at the zoo. But thinking of stories is something I'm good at.

Chapter 8   *Cleaning up*

Saturday, January 22nd. At six in the morning Joe and I walked along the Grand Concourse. It felt very cold again – winter was back. Joe had his gun inside his coat. As we passed Computer Kitchen we saw lights on inside. At the pet store it was dark inside, but I knew the door was unlocked. I could see light under the door to the back room. We went in and found Wilson and the Freemans.

"This is the big day," I said. "You know what to do, Mr. Freeman?"

"Yes," he replied. "Call the Grays, tell them my van won't start, and say I need to speak with them in their office."

After making the call, Freeman said, "They're really mad and want me in their office now."

"Good," I said. "Mr. Freeman, lock the street door behind us and stay in the back room."

In the street I gave Joe and Wilson gloves. "The NYPD must not know we've been in Computer Kitchen," I told them.

The street door to Computer Kitchen was unlocked. We went quietly up the stairs and stood in front of the office door.

"It's Freeman," said Wilson in a voice like his brother-in-law's. The door opened and we moved fast. Joe had his gun in his hands. I saw the beautiful furniture and expensive computers. On the desks were green and yellow bags from Freeman's store, and bags of drugs for the Grays' clients. The Grays didn't speak, but I could see they were afraid. I quickly stood on a chair and pulled the webcam from the wall.

"Move away from the desks and stand against the wall," Joe shouted to the Grays. "Put your hands on your heads …"

"A friend of Mr. Freeman wants to talk with you," I said.

Wilson's face looked the opposite of friendly as he moved around the desk. "Two good clean boys from Columbia University, huh?" he asked. "No, you're sick, dirty and dangerous. I'm going to hurt you for what you did to my family. We're going to put you out of business." Wilson looked down and said, "I'll start by cleaning your desks." With one arm he pushed the bags of drugs to the floor. Then he sat on the empty desk top and said, "That's what I call a clean desk. I hope …"

At that moment, Joe called from the window, "Boss, we got visitors!"

Outside in the street, four guys were getting out of a large black car. They were wearing sports clothes with hoods and carrying guns. It looked like the big boys were already here.

We had to move fast. "You boys, get down on the floor behind the desks!" I called to the Grays. "You too, Wilson. Joe, shoot high when I tell you. OK?"

Soon we heard feet on the stairs. Two guys with one gun can't fight against four all carrying guns. So I had to make sure our visitors couldn't count us. Joe and I were ready when the door flew open. As the first guy came in, I shouted loudly, "Police! Stop or we shoot! Now, Joe!"

Joe shot three times at the wall above the guy's head. I heard shouts from the stairs. "It's the cops! Get out of here!" Then we heard the noise of feet running down the stairs and onto the street. Car doors opened and shut and they drove away fast.

Wilson looked over the desk through the cloud of smoke and said, "Wow! That was like something from a movie."

"You got anything to say to us?" I asked the Grays. "Like 'Thank you we're not dead.'" There was no answer. They both looked white.

Now we had to move quickly. Maybe someone heard the shots. First, we had to get the Grays out of the way.

"We're going to help you leave town now," I went on. "Seattle, San Francisco, I don't mind where. We'll take you home to get a travel bag, then we're taking you to the airport. Joe, take these guys out to the car and wait for us there. Wilson and I have some cleaning up to do."

When Joe left with the Grays, we began our work.

"We have to do this carefully, Mr. Wilson. Find anything that could lead the police to Freeman, like his store bags," I said. "Leave all the drugs just where they are. I'm going to look for the webcam video."

Inside five minutes we had everything, including the webcam video. "Mr. Wilson, you take the pet store bags and put them on a fire someplace. But first, go and find Freeman and tell him what's happened. And help him clean the inside of his van from top to bottom. There must be nothing for the police to find."

We hurried downstairs to the street. Joe was waiting for me in his car with the Grays. Wilson walked back to Animals International, his head down against the snow.

The Grays lived at the northern end of Manhattan Island. Joe drove to their apartment and stopped outside.

"There's no need for you to come up," said Grant Gray.

"Really? I think there's every need," I said. "You have five minutes to get your things ready."

They started to walk up to their third-floor apartment. As I followed, Joe called me and I went back to the car.

"Boss," he said, "why are you letting these boys get away?"

I smiled. "Wait and see," I said. "I want them somewhere safe while Wilson and Freeman clean everything up. And where's safer than an airport?" Then I ran up the stairs to the Grays' apartment.

The front door was open and the lock was broken. At first, I could see nothing wrong inside, but then I saw it. Above a desk, behind a picture was a wall safe. The door was open and the safe was empty. On the wall was writing in large letters which read, 'WE KNOW WHERE YOU LIVE.' On the desk was blood and the body of a large dead snake – the Grays' Burmese python.

"Well, you boys do get a lot of friendly visitors. Someone's shot your pet snake and taken the drug money that you couldn't pay into the bank. Oh dear! I'm so sorry. Now move it and get your suitcases!" I shouted.

Chapter 9 *Thanks*

Joe drove the Grays to LaGuardia airport and I took a train back to Queens. It was time I finally had a day off. Sometimes I see too much of the dark side of this city. Now I could really use a rest.

But first there was just one more job for me to do. I went to Slim Pete's Diner for some breakfast and waited for Joe's call. After eggs, pancakes and bacon I felt like a new man.

Finally I got a call from Joe. "The Grays are waiting for a plane to San Francisco," he said.

"Thanks, Joe," I said. "We got the Grays just where we want them."

Now I had to call the police, but I did it from the pay phone in the diner. I didn't want to give the police my name or my cellphone number.

"I heard gun shots this morning from an office on the Grand Concourse in the Bronx," I said. "The place is Computer Kitchen, but I think you'll find drugs there if you go and look. The two guys who run the business are called Grant and Tyler Gray. They're waiting at LaGuardia for a plane to San Francisco. They'll be easy to find – they're blonde twins." I put the phone down before anyone could ask me questions. My job was done.

*   *   *

A few days later I got a call from Captain Oldenberg of the NYPD. I knew him from my time with the police.

"Marley, what are you up to?" he shouted. "What do you know about two guys called Gray with a drug business in the Bronx?"

"Nothing," I said, holding the phone away from my ear. "Why do you ask?"

"It's strange, Marley. They say you and another man with a gun visited their office," said Oldenberg, still shouting. "And another strange thing. We got a call from a diner in Queens. The caller told us where we could find the Grays. And the diner is someplace near your apartment, I think."

"As you say, Captain, all very strange," I replied.

Oldenberg said nothing for a minute. "I guess it's no good asking what you were doing there. But the important thing is we got the Grays, so the city streets are safer," he said at last. "And Marley, next time you know nothing about some of this city's bad guys, make sure you tell the police again."

*   *   *

On a fine spring morning in April, I got a letter from the Freemans. Inside was a photo of a happy little girl with a Kenyan sand boa snake in her hands. I remembered that snake – it was the one I nearly bought for my "son". The letter read:

Dear Mr. Marley,

We want to thank you for everything you did for us. We are now free to go on with our lives. It's truly wonderful to feel safe every day. Curtis lent us the money to help us with our problems and we're paying him back each month.

I can say that I have learned an important life lesson – to remember that your family is always there for you.
As you can see from the photo, your snake found a birthday girl.

Best regards,

Ellis and Dionne Freeman